Heart of Twigs

A collection of heartbreaks,
revelations, and contemplations on
unrequited situationships

Dedication

To Tom, whose constant and endearing artistic encouragement and support made this collection of dreams a reality.

Table of Contents

The Scientist

You scrambled my eggs
And percolated
Turkish coffee,
Breaking my fast
As you began yours.

I woke up
With your soccer jersey
Snatched at my waist,
Eager to see you clearly,
My modesty misplaced.

I was your Catwoman,
Asking all the wrong questions,
Letting all my lives die
Before your cautious eyes.

The daylight perforates
The holes we make at night,
The bashful dances that we steal
Between friends and spite.

You walked me
To the train,

Averting hands and eyes.

At 30th Street Station
You waved our first goodbye.

Braids 1

Waking and dreaming,
Still you flood my mind.

Your blue-jade eyes
Sparkle in delight
In the conjuring I see.

Your wide-tooth grin
Squinting dimples into crow's feet
In this vision of you and me.

Recurring wedding day fiascos,
Reception dances that melt into
Runaway promises.

Repeatedly,
Love requited,
Finally.

The Tops

You stand at the top of the steps
At the attic of my childhood home,
Ravaged by fire and flame –

In a charred, wooden landscape
You stand atop Mount Olympus,
The pearly gates reflected opal
In your summer-water eyes.

You are the tippy-top,
The pinnacle,
The peak and climax of it all.

Oh, I am terrified
Of the sight of your lips
Parted and panting,
Licked in anticipation
Of mine

You tower amidst the Gods,
You defend your heart with honor
You defend with grace -

You could never fall,

Nor falter from your pedestal on high -

How could you fall,
How could you falter
From that pedestal of mine?

Ours

You called it
Our hair
When I bleached
My ends
Raw –

Our hair
When I tinted
My highlights
Violet.

You call it
Our hands
When I make
A fist –

When I slam
The door.

But
You call it
My bed
When you stay
The night –

My walls
When I set
A borderline –

It's my future,
My home,
My money,
My time –

Ours is a pair
Of singular strands,
Crisscrossed intersections,
Parallel and perpendicular
Overlaid veils of grey matter gossamer.

Mine is a certainty of truth,
A material matter laid flat,
Dimensions diminished and
Cross sections drawn fast.

What is ours
Is always mine.

What is mine
Is not always ours.

Dark Academia

You called me lovely
From across the Atlantic,

With your baby blue
Button-up sleeves,
Rolled up, chivalrously frantic.

Hunched over a black-top desk,
Researching futures
And ironing out the specs –

Was it the microbes or robots
That kept you up at night?

Was it my forest-green eyes
Or the timid confidence that might
Have dully glowed like a night light?

You are just a memory,
Flitting to the foreground,
Swimming into view
When subtle rejection abounds.

You swung me around and

Tipsed me turvy,
But you dropped me to the ground
And found me unworthy.

Braids 2

Straight girls
Will never know the anguish
Of shared songs
Of inside jokes
Of borrowed clothes –

The proximity eludes them
The familiarity escapes them
The intimacy evades them –

Straight girls
Will never know the torture
Of a drunken kiss
Of a brushed-off-the-cheek eyelash
Of a hand-holding, tearful goodbye –

The depth of it baffles them
The intensity of it confuses them
The sweetness of it frightens them.

You are straight like an arrow,
Bending and flexing side to side
Against the wind on your tail.

You are straight like a whistle,
Gasping for air at every touch,
Shouting in alarm at every exhale.

Duped

The eyes
Of a newborn idol:
Sapphire shades
Buoyed by oceans
Of white,
Pedestaled high
Above the icons of old.

Grand
Were his lies,
Spectacular feats
Of wonderful esteem.

Deceived was I,
Sensationally displaced
In my own bleeding heart –

Deceived was I,
For wanting too hard.

Sunday Matinee

I am such a helpless romantic
That I want both
To be married
And
To be sleeping
With other people –

I want my love
Long,
I want my love
Soft,
I want my love
Calm.

But

I want my love
Fast,
I want my love
Fierce,
I want my love
Flaming.

I am such a reckless romantic

That I want none
Of the blame,
But
I will proudly proclaim
Your right
To my heart's domain.

Gorgeous, Gorgeous Girls

To be alone with you
To feel the soft plush
Of your alabaster integument –

To skim the surface
Of your ocean-deep intellect –

To satisfy your thirst,
To break your curse –

To be your reason
You chose girls –

I could be.

I would be.

Braids 3

I wish I could remember more
Of the moments when we were in love –

When you wrapped blue nail polish
In two rolls of Scotch tape
So that the bottle wouldn't break
On the ride in the school bus –

When we investigated a haunted house,
Sneaking out with the Mag Lites,
Trespassing in our field hockey kilts –

When you Skyped me the night
Before your flight
To make sure you packed
The right scarves for your semester away.

I wish I could remember more
Of the car rides to Border's,
Of the shoes we shared,
Of the yellow blouses you wore,
Of the ice cream pints under the winter's
full moon.

I wish I could remember more
Of the last nights together,
Before the fight outside the club,
Before you said you still loved him,
Before you tried to drunkenly kiss me –

I wish I could remember more
Of the days when you were mine.

Blue

He was opulent
Like the July Sky,
A baby-blue powder pastel,
Robin's egg in my eyes.

His smile radiated
Like the beams of the sun,
Yellow streams of summer
Down my back and bosom.

His hands warmed,
Wrapped around my heartstrings,
Pulled me closer
To his magnetic arch.

Like the dog days of summer,
Sweat beads racing down my neck,
His presence branded my soul
And stifled my breath.

Belonging was the sense
Of blue eyes and summer smiles,
Of coarse hands on soft necks –

Belonging was a sense
Of peace in the smog city park,
Of romance in a fraught friendship's knot
–

Belonging was the sense
Of fate interceding,
Of chances newly proceeding –

Blinded by faith in the powers of blue,
But mischief was there in plenty, too,
Revealing what once was scarce but true,
The fellow responds, "but not I you" –

For to gamble in the fate of love's divine
Is forsaking the truth that was not mine –
Soft words and hands are sweet and kind,
But treacherous, too, when stoked by
wine.

Wild Card

2 monogamous 10s,
1 polyamorous 9.

2 opposing sides
Straddle
1 fine line.

Messy

You tell me
We aren't messy enough
To cave in
To our desires,
To jump headfirst
Into each other's lips.

You chide me
For my longing looks
While we cry
To each other
About our lost youths.

You assure me
We will meet again
On our playground dreams,
Love never lost
Just
Love tearing at the seams.

Monuments

Pink and pruning petals
Falling gracefully in the breeze,
Poppyseed stamens strewn
Below the Lawn's trees -

Yet

You promised a paradise
Of forever dreams,
Of cherry blossom futures,
And romance supreme –

 You delivered on deals before,
 And championed on the playing pitch -

Yet

Broken promises litter,
Glitter my world,
Suppress my dreams in slumber,
Shake my life like thunder -

Yet

Monuments still stand erect,
My petals falling silently underfoot -

Abandoned promises linger still
In my sleeping daze,
Awaiting your arrival
Your homecoming, chaste.

Braids 4

If James Taylor
And Jack Johnson
Can call me back to your mind
After years there dormant –

After you tried to kiss me
A week before you met him –

After you married
On my birthday –

Where am I really?
Dormant
Or lingering?

Do his volunteering hours
Make you lonely?

Do you miss the excitement of life
Before motherhood stationed you?

Do you yearn for my longing stares,
Hunger for my melodramatic mania
To undermine your mature stability?

Do you regret letting me go,
Or despise the braided memories of our
youth?

Do you wish I'll come running
When you crawl back to me?

Exhumation

Sending the request
Was never
What I intended.

To be seen,
To be known
Was what I desired.

The push of a fingertip,
The twitch of a thumb pad,
Was all it took
To revive this need –

To be loved by you,
To be held by you,
To be healed by you.

Myriad schemes
I plotted
To keep you close,
None worthy
Of your choosing.

I dreamt of little Lottie Maes

With your sapphire eyes
And my untamed mane,

Of white-picket fences
And snowball fights,
Of Spanish wine tastings
And childish delights.

We lived these dreams
While you
Were with another.
In parallel forms,
We shared
These moments,
Allowing them
To hover.

Sending the request
Was never
What I intended –

Sending the request,
After six silent years,
Was only an
Alternative
To numbing
The dull and dying
Ache
I made for you here.

6 & One Half Dozen

The pain of seeing her smile without me,
In the hands of someone I don't know –

Betrayed,
Shunned,
Alone –

To be so full and so empty at the same
time –

Stuffed,
Comfy,
Overflowed –

Yet, she is soft,
She is gentle,
She is conviction,
Diligence,
Appetite,
Vigor –

Yet, as is he –

Were they to be the same soul,

I'd be none the wiser.

He builds me up,
She sails me away.

Summer Nights

It's the Florida nights
Of Girls Gone Wild
And excursions down the coast –

It's the pre-season days
Of sweaty camaraderie
And strict adherence to the Girl Code –

It's getting our first boyfriends
And never realizing how much detail
Is too much to know –

It's moving across the country
And never losing touch,
Never letting go –

It's swapping bags in the bathroom
And laughing off our asses,
But never saying no –

It's feeling the draw and pull,
You're feeling that draw and pull,
To pull her into the know –

So you slap on that smile
And you power through the pain –

There's never too much baggage, dear,
Never too much for me to claim.

Walk on down into the light
And settle into the sand,
Walk right in and sink down right,
I'll pick you out by hand,
I'll pick you every time.

Closure

I dream about closure,
Especially with you.
Closing the door on that chapter,
Shutting the window with no view.

I quiet the voice inside my head
That tells me to look back.
I white-knuckle the strength
And sideline my attacks.

Even now
I spiral
I spin
At the thought of you
At the glimpse of you
And what we could have been
What I dream should be.

But closure on a dream
Agonizingly left unrealized,

Is truly clarity
Begotten from divine intervention,
Saddled next to real-life interpretation.

Songbird

To you,
I will sing the sun's cries –

For you,
I would color the sunset's skies –

With you,
I could paint the ocean's rise –

But you,
I mourn,
Covet another's eyes –

Yet you,
Still here,
Hunger on your own lies.

Reflections

I lay my head
On your reflection,
Shining against the bus window,
Peering through lowered lids –

Never far from me
Are your tender hands.

I see your face
In every reflection.
I lay down my head,
Waiting for you discretion.

Never far from me,
Never too far for me.

Dreams lie always
That you'll choose me,
That he will flee –

Then why did you text –
Why
Did you break
The silence?

If perfect is what you have,
How am I not what you miss?

Haunting me
In my sleep,
Dreams
Play their tricks
That you'll choose me,
That you'll love me –

Unrequited
I stay,
Until the day
You come to me
Beneath the mango tree.

To Where

To wherever you are,
Under the mango tree,
Or at the Women's March,
Swapping notes
Or creating art,
You bookend my romantic spark –

To there where you are,
Inside a log cabin,
Or at Bryant Park,
Writing poems
Or journaling in the dark,
You ignited my romantic heart –

To here where you aren't,
Outside the Jewel Osco,
Or at South Ab Park,
Creating a dream
Or stealing my heart,
You disturbed by romantic parts –

To where I won't be,
Inside your swing class,
Or converting to make is easy,

Competing for worthiness
Or making me seem less dreamy,
You trampled my romantic heart.

Heart of Twigs

Katie at 6 didn't know the rules,
Wasn't handed the instructions,
And met imaginary friends after school.

At 8, she learned to play the game,
Couldn't find the right speed,
But tried just the same.

At 10, she had transferred 2 schools,
Just couldn't find the right fit,
But slowly concepting all the rules.

At 12, she'd cried out her heart,
Abandoned the game,
And proudly wrote her sing-song art.

At 14, she was under his thumb,
Wrote letters to read nevermore,
And started to feel the numb.

At 16, she had a hefty scare,
Slept more than ever before,
And just had to get out of there.

Katherine at 18 left for university,

Changed her name,
And begged for someone else to be.

KT in college lost her way around,
Read between the blurry lines,
And abandoned a dream downtown.

At 22, she couldn't figure out
Whether she was hopeful still
Or flinging herself about.

At 25, she got engaged,
Struggled in the day-to-day,
Convinced she'd never catch a break.

At 28, life had a new landscape,
She flourished in Chicago,
Feeling her world slowly reshape.

Kat at 30 wears her weight well,
And she courts her fate,
But she cannot foretell.

The Katies of the future
Can't wait to read the lines,
Perform some more and get a gig,
And heal her tender heart of twigs.

Acknowledgements

Where would I be without you: Casey, Cheryl, Bryce, Meki, Meghan, Leah, Cindy, Tom, Dad, Tammy, and Andrew. You all lifted me up and encouraged me to keep writing, to keep moving forward, during the darkest times of my life. I am graciously indebted to you all.

About the Author

Katie Taylor was born in Scranton, Pennsylvania, and was raised in the wooded township of Waverly, PA. A poet by nature, she attended the Writer's Institute at Susquehanna University. In 2019, she moved to Chicago, where she has flourished amid the creative and professional scenes. While composing "Heart of Twigs," Katie also compiled three more chapbooks she hopes to publish in the coming years.